# DEMOCRATIC VALUES
## A Kid's Guide

by Cari Meister

CAPSTONE PRESS
a capstone imprint

Captivate is published by Capstone Press, an imprint of Capstone.
1710 Roe Crest Drive,
North Mankato, Minnesota 56003
www.capstonepub.com

Library of Congress Cataloging-in-Publication data is available on the Library
of Congress website.
ISBN 978-1-5435-9141-5 (library binding)
ISBN 978-1-4966-6605-5 (paperback)
ISBN 978-1-5435-9145-3 (eBook PDF)

Summary: Facts about democratic values and how they play a part in
U.S. elections.

**Image Credits**
Alamy: Hero Images Inc., 23, (bottom), North Wind Picture Archives, 10, P&F
Photography, 4, RosaIreneBetancourt 6, 15, (middle), Tony Tallec, 22; iStockphoto:
adamkaz, 14, CastaldoStudio, 11, RichLegg, 21; Shutterstock: Anne Kitzman, 17, dani
shlom, 9, Dasha Rosato, 16, David Pereiras, 24, 29, Jim Ekstrand, 27, KeyStock, 12,
Monkey Business Images, 18, 19, 23, (middle and top), 26, mooremedia, 25, NATNN,
15, (bottom), Rawpixel.com, 6, 15, (top), Rob Crandall, 8, sre11, 20, vladwel, Cover,
wavebreakmedia, 5, WAYHOME studio, 28; Wikimedia: Cecil Stoughton, White
House Press Office, 13, Official White House Photo by Joyce N. Boghosian, 7

**Design Elements**
Capstone; Shutterstock: openeyed, GarganTul

**Editorial Credits**
Editor: Michelle Parkin; Designer: Bobbie Nuytten;
Media Researcher: Jo Miller; Production Specialist: Laura Manthe

Printed in the United States of America.
PA99

# Table of Contents

Glossary terms are **bold** on first use.

★ ★ ★ ★ ★ ★ ★ ★ ★ ★ ★ ★ ★ ★

# What Is a Democratic Value?

During election time, you may hear people talking about **values**. But what are values? A value is a belief that is based on what you think is right. For example, let's say someone values honesty. What does honesty mean to you? Imagine it's raining outside. You spend school recess running around and having fun. When you come back in, your shoes are covered in mud. You forget to wipe them on the mat and track brown mud all over your classroom.

If you do something wrong at school, be honest and tell your teacher.

Your teacher says that the person who made the mess needs to help clean it up. You know it was you, but you don't want to clean the floor. What do you do? If you value honesty, you tell the truth about what you did. This value is important to you.

Democratic values are beliefs that people share in a **society**. **Liberty**, **equality**, and being a good **citizen** are all democratic values. Let's take a closer look at what they are and what they mean to you.

A society is made up of many different people.

**FACT:** The word *democracy* comes from the Greek words *demos* and *kratos*. Demos means "people." Kratos means "power."

## WE ALL HAVE A SAY

In the United States, our government is based on **democracy.** That means that the people have a say in how the government is run. How? We **vote** for the leaders who share our values. The people we vote for represent us in government.

Government leaders gather at the U.S. Capitol to make decisions for our country.

# Liberty

Liberty is an important democratic value. Liberty means freedom. In the United States, you have the freedom to believe what you want. You have the freedom to choose what religion to follow. You have the freedom to form your own ideas and opinions.

People attended a protest in Washington, D.C.

Protestors stood outside the White House in 2019.

You are also free to share your ideas with others. You can write what you think in a blog. You can go to a protest and stand up against things you disagree with. Other people have these freedoms too. It's important to let people follow their own beliefs, even if they are different from yours.

The idea of liberty goes back to when this nation was founded. Before the United States was a country, it was a **colony** of Great Britain. American colonists wanted to separate from Great Britain. They wanted their own country. They didn't want to be ruled by a king. As a result, colonists fought against the British in the Revolutionary War (1775–1783). The colonists won.

Early leaders wrote down values they wanted people in our society to follow.

Our early leaders wrote down values they wanted in society. These democratic values are in important documents, such as the U.S. **Constitution**.

The U.S. Constitution

# Equality and Individual Rights

Equality is another democratic value. Equality means that everyone is treated as equals. It shouldn't matter how much money you have, where you live, what religion you practice, or what color your skin is. Our country has laws to protect equality. For example, an employer cannot fire someone based on age or gender.

You cannot be fired from your job because of things like gender, age, or race.

Why is equality important in a society? People feel connected to their community if they are accepted. People who feel connected help their communities grow and succeed.

**FACT:** According to the Civil Rights Act of 1964, it is against the law to treat someone differently based on race, religion, gender, or where they are from.

President Lyndon Johnson signed the Civil Rights Act into law.

All U.S. citizens have the same individual **rights**. The Constitution guarantees certain rights. For example, citizens who are at least 18 years old have the right to vote.

A woman votes during Election Day.

Let's look at some other rights:

**Freedom of Speech:** You have the right to say what you think without being stopped or punished. For example, if you disagree with something our government is doing, you have the right to say something and to tell others about it.

**Freedom of the Press:** You have the right to write your ideas and beliefs. This is also important for journalists and other members of the media. The government cannot stop them from printing stories, even if it makes the government look bad.

**Freedom of Religion:** You have the right to practice the religion you choose. You have the right to switch religions or not belong to any religion. The government cannot treat one religious group better than another.

# Civic Duties

For our government to work well, we all have to take an active role in our communities. This means that everyone needs to do their civic duty. That means you too!

So, what are civic duties? Civic duties are rules we follow that help our country and the people who live here. This includes obeying the laws. You are doing your civic duty each time you go to school. The law says you have to attend school until you reach a certain age. When you ride your bike, you do your civic duty by wearing your helmet and following bike safety rules on the street.

Do your civic duty and wear a helmet when riding your bike.

Sometimes there are penalties for not doing your civic duty. For example, someone could get a fine for driving faster than the posted speed limit. If someone steals something from a store, that person could get arrested.

Drivers can receive tickets and pay fines for not obeying traffic laws.

It is also our civic duty to follow rules at home, in school, and around our communities. These rules may not be laws, but they are still important. Like laws, rules are made to keep everyone safe. At school, your teacher may tell you not to run in the hallways. This rule helps keep you and people around you from falling and getting hurt.

Follow the rules at school, such as walking in the halls.

Rules are also put into place to help make your community a good place to live. Cities and counties have their own rules that people need to follow. For example, a city could have a rule that all dogs need to be leashed when in public. If someone doesn't follow that rule, that person could be fined.

Follow the laws in your city, such as keeping dogs leashed in public.

A driver must follow the traffic laws, such as stopping for people on crosswalks.

Adults have to do their civic duty too. They have to file taxes every year. People who drive on public roads have to follow traffic laws.

Another civic duty for adults is to serve on a jury. A jury is a group of people who votes on whether or not a person is guilty of a crime. In the United States, it is a person's responsibility to serve on a jury if asked. Voting is also an important civic duty for adults. It is how we make changes in our government.

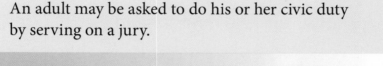

An adult may be asked to do his or her civic duty by serving on a jury.

# Be a Good Citizen

Being a good citizen is kind of like playing on a sports team. On a sports team, you have to work with your teammates and be respectful to the other team. Good citizens have to work together as a community and respect others. Then everyone wins. Citizens should be honest, respectful, cooperative, and help those around them.

Be a good citizen and respect people around you.

So how do you do these things?

**Be respectful.** At school, be kind to people who think, look, learn, or act differently from you. Listen to your teachers, raise your hand in class, and wait until teachers call on you to answer. Clean up your lunch tray when you are finished eating.

**Be honest.** Being honest means telling the truth. If you tell your mom you took out the trash, make sure you did. Finish your homework before you tell your dad it is done.

**Be cooperative.** Being cooperative means working well with others. When you are assigned a group project at school, work together as a team. Listen to others without speaking over them. Consider another person's point of view, even if it's different from your own. When everyone works together, you all end up with a great experience and a good grade.

# What You Can Do

You may have heard your parents and neighbors talk about ways to make your community even better. Maybe you have ideas too. Guess what? You can help! Our communities are much stronger when everyone pitches in and helps to make them better.

You can volunteer to pick up trash in a community park.

Volunteer. Look for ways to help those around you. Spend some time helping in your community. You could collect money for a worthy cause or run a marathon for something you believe in. You can help an elderly neighbor shovel his or her driveway in winter or mow the lawn in summer. It all makes a difference.

You can help neighbors by shoveling snowy driveways.

Talk to your friends and family about what matters to them. Encourage them to be good citizens as well. Ask them to come with you when you are volunteering, or find another way they can help the community.

Talk to your friends about volunteering with you in your community.

Learn about issues that interest you. Do you want to know more about climate change? Are you interested in recycling? Go online and learn all about the issues that you care about. Sometimes, people have opinions for or against certain topics. It's important to get the facts and learn both sides of an issue you feel strongly about.

Treat others how you would like to be treated, especially those who don't agree with you.

Research issues that interest you online.

## Stand Up!

Are you passionate about keeping plastics out of our oceans? Maybe you think the government should fund more space exploration. Whatever your passion, stand up, speak up, and help. Write a letter to a government leader such as a state **representative**. Invite friends to discuss ways to get involved, or simply help someone in need.

Write a letter to your representative about an issue that you are passionate about.

## Hooray for Democratic Values!

Our government is based on some amazing democratic values. It is up to you to help support them. Be a good citizen and help others be good citizens too. The better each of us does, the better our country will do as a whole.

# Glossary

**citizen** (SI-tuh-zuhn)—a member of a country or state who has the right to live there

**colony** (KAH-luh-nee)—an area that has been settled by people from another country

**Constitution** (kon-stuh-TOO-shun)—a written system of laws that states the rights of the people and powers of the U.S. government

**democracy** (di-MAH-kruh-see)—a form of government where the people can choose their leaders

**equality** (i-KWAH-luh-tee)—the same rights for everyone

**liberty** (LIB-ur-tee)—freedom from control

**right** (RITE)—something that the law says you can have or do

**representative** (rep-ri-ZEN-tuh-tiv)—a person elected to serve the government; U.S. representatives serve in the House of Representatives

**society** (suh-SYE-uh-tee)—a group that shares the same laws and customs

**value** (VAL-yoo)—a belief or idea that is important to a person

**vote** (VOHT)—to make a choice in an election

# Read More

Berne, Emma Carlson. *Understanding How You Can Help.* North Mankato, MN: Capstone Press, 2018.

Raatma, Lucia. *Citizenship.* Ann Arbor, MI: Cherry Lake Pub., 2014.

Turner, Joshua. *The Purpose of Rules and Laws.* New York: PowerKids Press, 2018.

# Internet Sites

*Ben's Guide to the U.S. Government*
https://bensguide.gpo.gov/

*Civic Engagement*
https://youth.gov/youth-topics/civic-engagement-and-volunteering

*PBS Kids: You Choose*
https://pbskids.org/youchoose

# Index